Into the A, B, Sea

AN OCEAN ALPHABET

BY **DEBORAH LEE ROSE**   PICTURES BY **STEVE JENKINS**

SCHOLASTIC PRESS · NEW YORK

Swim the ocean waves with me

and dive into the A, B, Sea

where Anemones sting

and Barnacles cling

where Crabs crawl in

and Dolphins spin

where Eels explore

and Flying fish soar

where Gray whales peep

and Humpbacks leap

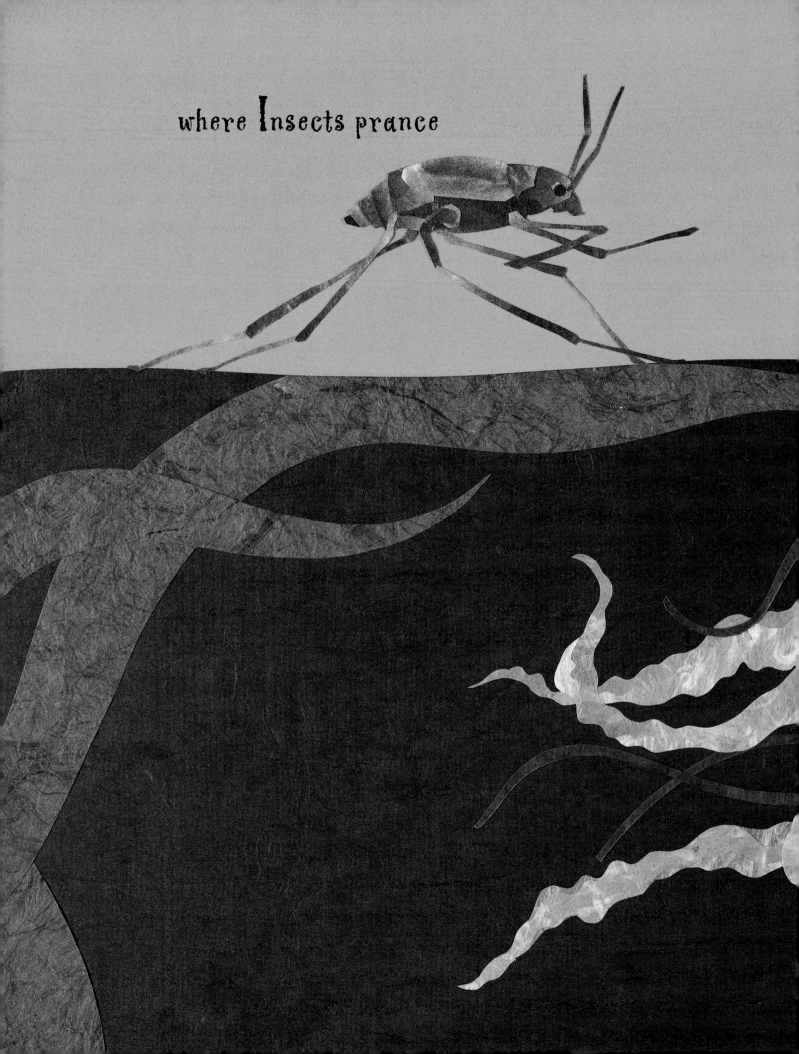

where Insects prance

and Jellies dance

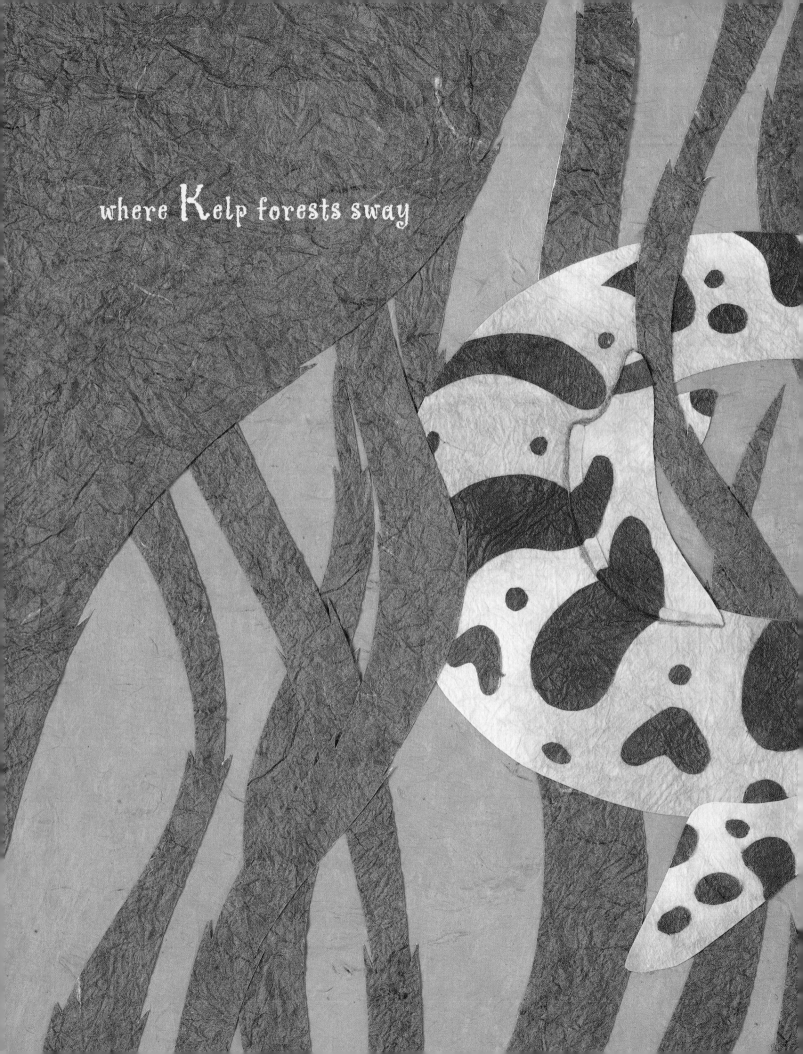

where Kelp forests sway

and Leopard sharks prey

where Manatees lumber

and Narwhals slumber

where Octopuses hide

and Penguins glide

where Queen angels glow

and Rays swoop low

where Sea stars grab

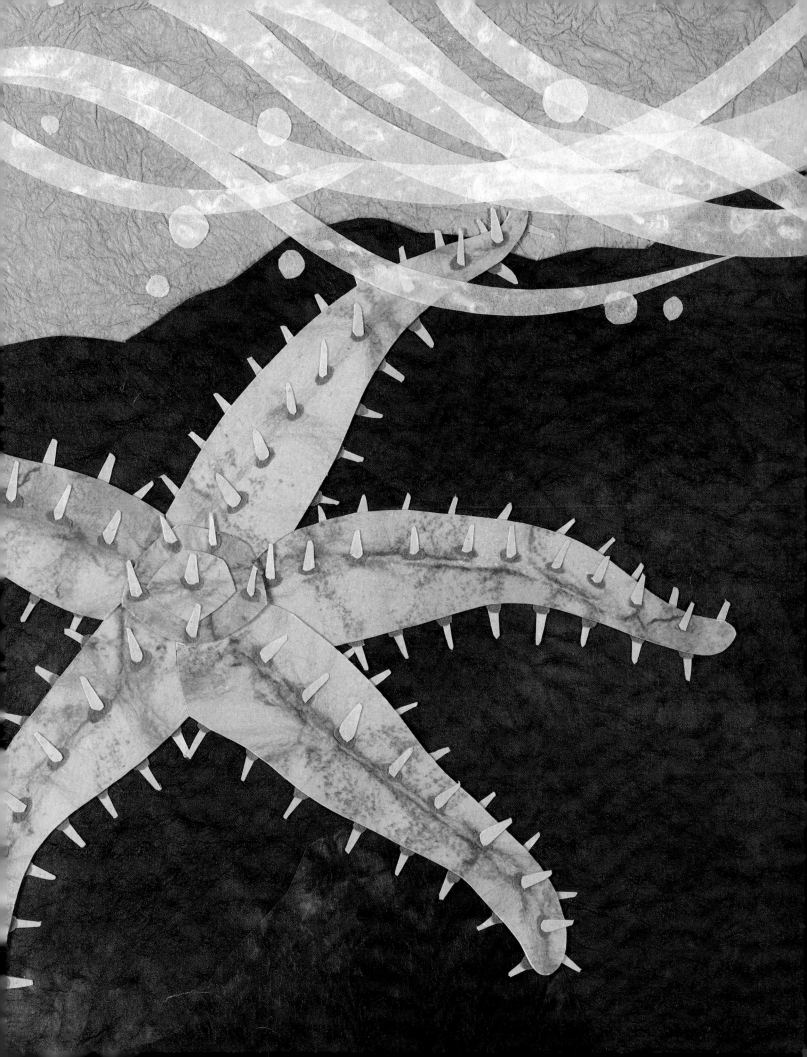

and Tiger sharks nab

and Viperfish shine

where blue Whales eXhale

where Yellowfin dive

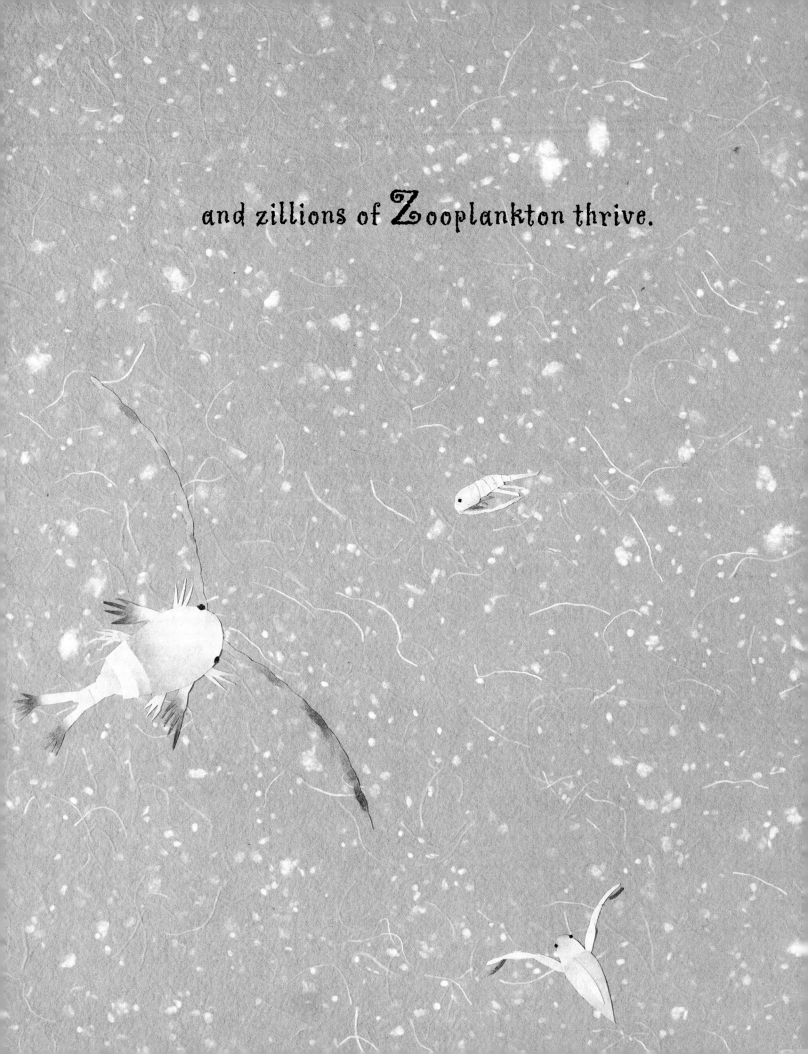

and zillions of Zooplankton thrive.

Now come and swim again with me

through the wonders of the A, B, Sea!

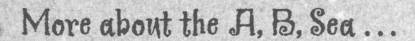

More about the A, B, Sea . . .

ANEMONES STING: Anemones (uh-*neh*-moh-neez) look like flowers blooming on the coral reef, but they are really animals. They stun their prey with poisonous tentacles, though some creatures, like clownfish, can hide safely among them.

BARNACLES CLING: Barnacles make their own kind of "superglue" to stick to rocks, ships, fishing piers, the skin of whales, and snail and turtle shells. Once barnacles stick, their hold is so strong even the roughest weather may not knock them off.

CRABS CRAWL IN: Hermit crabs don't make the shell homes they carry around with them, but use empty shells left by other creatures that have died. As hermit crabs grow bigger, they are always searching for the "perfect" new house to fit their size and shape.

DOLPHINS SPIN: Spinner dolphins are the ocean's best gymnasts, twirling and somersaulting high over the waves before falling gracefully back into the sea. Underwater, dolphins use *echolocation*, like bats, sending out special sound waves to help them "see."

EELS EXPLORE: Eels slither like snakes, or lurk among rocks and coral to catch fish and octopuses by surprise. Some eels can lock their jaws around their prey, then tear off pieces for food using their very sharp teeth.

FLYING FISH SOAR: Flying fish fling themselves out of the sea and glide through the air on their fins to escape from predators. When these fish "fly," hungry squid, dolphins, and larger fish often lose sight of them and give up the chase.

GRAY WHALES PEEP: Gray whales *spyhop* by poking just their heads out of the ocean to take a good look around. These gentle giants travel thousands of miles from cold polar seas, where they feed, to warm tropics, where they give birth to their young.

HUMPBACKS LEAP: Humpbacks and other whales *breach* by hurling themselves over the waves and splashing down on the sea like thunder. As they float in the water, male humpbacks create some of the most intricate songs sung by any animal.

INSECTS PRANCE: Countless insects burrow in the sand and hover over seaweed where the ocean meets the sandy beach and rocky shore. Marine water striders are unusual because they are found on the open sea, where they lay eggs on floating kelp or driftwood, and feed on dead jellies.

JELLIES DANCE: Jellies, or jellyfish, drift on the ocean currents, trapping small prey with stinging tentacles or sticky mucus. They seem to dance as their sac-like bells pulse rhythmically, filling with sea water, emptying, and filling again.

KELP FORESTS SWAY: Giant kelp grows very fast — sometimes a foot a day. Tall, thick kelp forests provide plenty of food and hiding places for darting fish, scrambling crabs, crawling snails, diving shorebirds, and frolicking sea otters and seals.

LEOPARD SHARKS PREY: Leopard sharks cruise the kelp forest, searching for crabs and fish to chomp with their three-pointed teeth. Speckled bands on their gray skin keep them camouflaged until they're ready to pounce.

MANATEES LUMBER: Manatees must live in warm waters, since their bulky bodies have little fat to insulate them. Munching for hours on water plants, manatees sometimes seem to tiptoe on their stubby front flippers.

NARWHALS SLUMBER: Narwhals (nar-walz) are called "unicorns of the sea" because in males, one front tooth grows into a long, spiraled tusk. These whales swim deep in cold Arctic waters and may get trapped by ice when winter comes.

OCTOPUSES HIDE: Octopuses have three hearts and blue blood and can grow a new arm if one of their eight gets eaten. They hide by squirting out an octopus-shaped cloud of ink, or by changing color instantly to blend in with their environment.

PENGUINS GLIDE: Penguins are birds that can't fly in the air, but they are fantastic swimmers! On land they waddle, hop, or slide to the ocean's edge, then dive in and flap their wings to "fly" through the water.

QUEEN ANGELS GLOW: Queen angelfish gleam as they nibble sea sponges made of millions of tiny animals. Older queen angels wear shining "crowns" of bright blue scales on their foreheads.

RAYS SWOOP LOW: With fins like wings, rays hover over the sandy ocean floor, protecting themselves with their stinging tails. Some rays make their own electricity to shock their food before they devour it.

SEA STARS GRAB: Sea stars, or starfish, hold tight to slippery rocks when giant waves crash over them. Some stars have five arms, and some have more than twenty. An entire new star can grow from one severed arm, if part of the original sea star's body is still attached.

TIGER SHARKS NAB: Tiger sharks tear and swallow almost anything, just like great white sharks. Rows of jagged teeth fill the shark's jaws, so if any fall out there are plenty left for biting.

UMBRELLAMOUTHS DINE: Umbrellamouth gulpers live in water so deep that sunlight never reaches them, and prey are few and far between. Gulpers grab whatever food they can find, even if it is larger than they are, and stash it in their huge mouths to swallow later.

VIPERFISH SHINE: Viperfish attack with long, sharp fangs to survive in deep water where food is scarce. At night they follow other fish to the surface, flashing their body lights to attract tasty victims.

BLUE WHALES EXHALE: Whales are mammals, like people, and must come to the surface for air. When whales breathe out through their *blowholes*, the warm exhaled air spouts high above the ocean. The spout shape depends on what kind of whales they are.

YELLOWFIN DIVE: Powerful and fast, yellowfin tuna race under the water in *schools* of thousands of fish. With dolphins by their side, the tuna can churn up large surfaces of the sea with their golden fins.

ZOOPLANKTON THRIVE: Zooplankton (zo-uh-plank-ton) are the ocean's tiniest animals, but they make a great meal for blue whales — the largest creatures that have ever lived in the sea or anywhere on earth.

FOR BENJAMIN, WHO LOVES THE SEA —D. L. R.

FOR JAMIE, ALEC, AND PAGE —S. J.

The author wishes to thank Marine Activities, Resources & Education (MARE), U.C.-Berkeley Lawrence Hall of Science, especially Catherine Halversen, Co-Director, who offered expert advice in the making of this book; the Monterey Bay Aquarium; and the National Oceanic and Atmospheric Administration (NOAA), whose ongoing efforts in ocean conservation, education, and public awareness helped inspire this book. These groups and others, such as the National Marine Educators Association, provide an "ocean" of resources for teachers, librarians, and readers of all ages.

Text copyright © 2000 by Deborah Lee Rose • Illustrations copyright © 2000 by Steve Jenkins • All rights reserved. • Published by Scholastic Press, an imprint of Scholastic Inc., *Publishers since 1920.* SCHOLASTIC, SCHOLASTIC PRESS, and associated logos are trademarks and/or registered trademarks of Scholastic Inc. • Library of Congress Cataloging-in-Publication Data available. Library of Congress number: 99-050034 • ISBN 0-439-09696-0 • 15 14 13 12 11 10   0/08 09 10 11 Printed in Singapore • 46 • First edition, September 2000 • The illustrations for this book are cut-paper collages. The type in this book was set in Greymantle, Cleanhouse, and Dogma. • Book design by Marijka Kostiw